Science Fair Showdown!

written by Steven Otfinoski
illustrated by Violet Lemay

HILLSDALE HIGH SCHOOL
SCIENCE FAIR
• FIRST PLACE •

PEARSON

Glenview, Illinois • Boston, Massachusetts • Chandler, Arizona
New York, New York

PEARSON

ISBN-13: 978-0-328-87262-6
ISBN-10:   0-328-87262-8
1 2 3 4 5 6 7 8 9 10   20 19 18 17 16

Contents

The NOBLE GASES
make up GROUP 18
in the periodic table

helium (HE
neon (NE)
argon (A

4

CHAPTER 1

A Winning Idea

Albert, Diya, and Sofia sat together in homeroom, discussing their science fair project. The three high-school sophomores had been friends since kindergarten and teamed up for major projects whenever they had the chance. Working together made everything easier and more fun.

"I think this will be great!" said Albert. "The impact of human activities on the Arctic is timely and compelling, so people will really be interested."

"Absolutely," agreed Diya, tossing her braid back over her shoulder. "And we've already done most of the preliminary research."

"Yeah," chimed in Sofia, "and we have a month to put the project together. Plenty of time! First place, here we come!"

As the bell rang to signal the end of homeroom, the three friends headed out the door and into the crowded halls of Hillsdale High.

"I think Mr. K is going to ask us for our project ideas today," said Diya as they ambled into chemistry class, taking their seats in the back row. Mr. Kowalski, their teacher and the chairperson of the annual science fair, asked the class to settle down. He was a popular teacher, with the gift of making difficult aspects of chemistry lucid and entertaining to his students.

"I've got an important announcement to make," he said. "As most of you know, the science fair will be held next month, and this year we're going to do things a little differently. For the first time, the fair will have a theme. The science faculty believes this will inspire you to do great things. The theme is *Using Science to Improve Our Community*."

Albert's face fell, Diya let out a groan, and Sofia furrowed her brow. They knew that their idea of a project about Arctic habitats hardly fit into that category.

"We live in several different communities," Mr. Kowalski continued, "including our neighborhoods, our town, and our high school. How can we use science to improve people's lives in one or more of these communities? Think it over and submit your project ideas to me by next Friday for approval. Any questions?"

As a couple of students asked questions about possible projects, Sofia sank back in her seat with a sigh. She had been up late three nights in a row researching Arctic climate change online. Now all her work was wasted. *Our Arctic idea just melted into a pool of slush*, she thought.

Diya, who always got anxious when plans went awry, tried to think of a solution without panicking. Was there a way to connect the Arctic to their own community? Could they perhaps do something with the polar bear exhibit at the zoo? *No*, she

thought, crestfallen. *We aren't third graders.*
We need something more sophisticated.

Albert, ever resourceful, whispered to his
partners, "How about recycling? That sure
fits with the theme. And I know people in
our neighborhood who still don't recycle. We
could show how increasing recycling would
help the community. In fact—"

He was interrupted as Keith and Kevin
Espinoza spoke up together from the front
row. The twin brothers were the top science
students in the sophomore class, always
making top-notch presentations.

"Can we do our project on recycling, Mr. Kowalski?" asked Keith.

"Community recycling," added Kevin. "We hope to show how recycling reduces garbage, improves the environment, and contributes to new manufacturing jobs in our community."

"That's an excellent idea, gentlemen," said Mr. Kowalski. "It sounds like you have it planned out. But just make sure I see a written proposal by next Friday."

Albert scowled. The twins had a long streak of winning every science prize, mainly because their mother was a research scientist and their father was good at building things. Of course, to be fair, the twins really were smart and clever with their science projects, especially Keith. At last year's science fair, he somehow proved that the chicken came before the egg.

"Well," Albert sighed aloud to his two partners, "we'll just have to think of something else."

Mr. Kowalski looked over at Albert. "Mr. Carney, would you like to share your project idea with the rest of us?"

"Well, our idea doesn't fit the new theme," replied Albert, embarrassed. "Sofia, Diya, and I have to figure out a new plan."

"In that case," said Mr. Kowalski, "everyone please open up your textbooks to page 52. We'll review the noble gases on the periodic table."

"Let's brainstorm during study period in the library," whispered Sofia to her two friends. "Meet at the long table by the computers."

CHAPTER 2

Back to the Drawing Board

Albert, Diya, and Sofia sat glumly and silently at the big library table. Albert's eyes were half-closed in thought, Sofia was doodling in her notebook, and Diya picked anxiously at her eraser.

"I bet the Espinozas are out there right now collecting cardboard boxes and making them into little recycled apartments for stray kittens," grumbled Sofia.

Diya laughed at this image, but Albert looked discouraged. "I don't have the energy for jokes right now. Can we please stay focused on—" he began.

"Energy! That's it!" Sofia exclaimed, causing Ms. Melrose, the librarian, to shush her indignantly from across the room.

"The world is running out of fossil fuels," Sofia went on more quietly. "We can do a project on renewable, clean energy sources that improve the community because they don't cause pollution!"

Albert and Diya nodded slowly as the idea took hold. "Everybody's interested in renewable energy these days," Diya agreed.

"And it's something we can demonstrate," said Albert thoughtfully. "The Espinoza twins won't be able to actually recycle something in their exhibit. But we can *show* how renewable energy works. Now, what kind of renewable energy should we focus on? Let's split up for fifteen minutes to do a little research and thinking. Then we'll compare notes."

Sofia, always a decisive and quick thinker, didn't have to consult a single reference source. An idea came to her right away. They could build a small wind turbine, just big enough to generate electricity to power a light bulb. *It wouldn't have to be 20 stories high like those giant turbines near the highway,* she thought. Picking up her pencil, Sofia began sketching a diagram of her wind turbine.

Diya had started to walk toward the reference shelves, but paused halfway there as a memory stirred. *What about solar panels?* she thought. The Wilsons, who lived next door to Diya, had solar panels on their roof. Maybe Albert and Sofia would agree to a project showing how to improve the neighborhood by using more solar energy! After all, the sun's power was limitless. When Diya had last babysat for Annie Wilson, the little girl had told her the solar panels provided electricity for the Wilsons' entire house.

Fired with excitement about her idea, Diya went back to the table and began writing up a plan for the project. She knew it would take a good, well-reasoned outline to convince Albert and Sofia, both of whom always had strong opinions of their own. Diya was usually content to let one of the others take the lead in ideas and decisions. But this time she was sure her plan could win them the coveted first prize.

Glancing up from the encyclopedia he'd been reading on his laptop, Albert saw that Sofia was busy drawing diagrams, and Diya's fingers were racing over her laptop keyboard. *I'd better come up with something quick!* he thought. Just then, a roaring engine disturbed the silence of the library, as a car sped by outside. *That's it!* thought Albert. It suddenly came to him that the biggest environmental problem was the millions of cars on the road. They could do a project showing what effect it would have on the community if gasoline were replaced with a clean, renewable fuel.

Albert turned back to his laptop and looked up *biofuel.* Soon he was reading about the different types of fuel that come from organic sources, such as the used french-fry oil from the diner on Newton Street, where he and his cousin Billy used to race remote-controlled cars. Albert learned that the diner was no longer dumping its used oil. Instead, it was selling it to be made into fuel.

To make biofuel, he read, plant matter or vegetable oil was treated, mixed with a little gasoline, and poured into a gas tank. Albert thought this sounded pretty simple. Suddenly he knew how to make his idea into a project. Uncle Phil, with whom Albert had lived since he was seven, owned an auto repair shop. *He must know all about this stuff,* thought Albert, becoming more and more excited by his own idea. *I bet Uncle Phil can help us turn this idea into a prize-winning project!*

Albert leaned back in his seat, momentarily carried away by a beautiful daydream of accepting the first prize as the Espinozas looked on enviously. Just for once, it sure would feel good to come in ahead of those two!

When the fifteen minutes were up, the three friends regrouped at the table.

Before anyone else said anything, Sofia declared, "Let's build a wind turbine!"

"A wind turbine?" echoed Diya. "Why don't we just build a nuclear reactor while we're at it?"

"I'm talking about making a single light bulb work," said Sofia. "It wouldn't be that ginormous."

"Well, I think we should do something with solar energy," Diya said. "It's practically limitless."

Sofia wasn't impressed. "Wind power is limitless too. There's no end to our supply of wind."

"But," said Diya, "there's not so much wind on a calm day."

"And solar power doesn't have limits? Have you ever heard of clouds?" countered Sofia. "Or night?"

Albert laid his hands, palms down, on the table. "Look," he said. "We need to address one of the most pressing energy problems we have today."

Sofia gave Albert a cold stare. "OK, Albert Einstein, what's your idea?"

Albert leaned forward dramatically. "I'm thinking about biofuel," he said, "to replace gasoline. My uncle can probably help us get some biofuel."

Sofia rolled her eyes and the three friends argued in whispers. For once they could not agree. Finally Sofia pushed back her chair in exasperation.

"This is going nowhere fast, and Keith and Kevin have probably built a whole house out of used cell phone batteries by now," she said. "How about if we all go home and develop our ideas? We can meet up again a week from today and present what we've done. The best one will be the choice for our project."

"That sounds good to me," said Albert, closing his laptop.

"Me too," agreed Diya. "But we'd better not meet in the library again, 'cause I don't think Ms. Melrose appreciates all the chattering."

"This is getting exciting," said Sofia, rising from the table. "May the best energy source win!"

CHAPTER 3

Making It Work

"Here's your biofuel," said Albert's uncle Phil, holding a jar of honey-colored liquid up to the light in the garage. "This is called ethanol."

"Thanks for your help, Uncle Phil! Is it really just corn oil?" asked Albert.

"It's fermented corn oil. Most gasoline already has a little added ethanol, and ethanol-based biofuel has a little bit of gasoline," explained Uncle Phil as he pulled containers from the refrigerator and began preparing dinner. "Oil, coal, and fossil fuels are biofuels too. But they were made millions of years ago from dead plants and animals. This jar of ethanol came from plants living today."

While Uncle Phil reheated last night's leftover Irish stew, Albert set the table. He listened with interest as Uncle Phil told him about other biofuels based on sunflower oil and soybean oil, and—Albert's personal favorite—a Brazilian fuel based on sugar cane! Even animal fat had proved a viable basis for biofuel.

"This is excellent background info for our project," Albert said. "But I need to figure out a way to demonstrate how biofuel works."

Uncle Phil offered to lend him a small motor from the shop. "I'll leave it out in the garage for you to pick up when you get home from school," he told Albert.

Looks like we'll be going with my idea, Albert congratulated himself. As he attacked his bowl of stew, he relished the thought of how impressed Sofia and Diya would be when he presented his working engine running on biofuel.

Meanwhile, over at the Martinez house, Sofia told her parents about her idea.

"You're going to build a wind turbine?" Mr. Martinez asked incredulously. "Like those monstrosities near the highway?"

Sofia laughed at the idea of a high-school sophomore building a real, full-size wind turbine. She explained that she had done research online and found simple plans to make a small, portable system that would work in the backyard. "After all," she told her parents, "I'm only trying to get a light bulb to work, not power all of downtown!"

Mrs. Martinez looked up from her dinner plate. "Why don't you show us your plans and ideas after we finish eating?" she suggested. "Maybe we can help you build your wind turbine."

Sofia hesitated. She always felt pleased at her parents' genuine interest in her schoolwork, but on the other hand she was very independent. She explained that the rules of the science fair required that students do the work themselves. But adult guidance was welcome, she hastened to add.

"OK," grinned Mrs. Martinez. "Then we'll supervise!"

As usual, Sofia had neatly organized her notes and ideas. She showed her parents the directions she had downloaded from the Internet and the parts she would need: a generator or motor, blades that would turn in the wind, a mounting and a hub for the blades, a tower to raise the mounting high enough to catch enough wind, and an electrical control system with batteries to convert the wind energy into electricity.

"We can probably buy the motor and electrical supplies online," said Sofia's father,

sitting down next to her and looking over her shoulder at her open laptop. Together, they looked at an electronics site that offered small motors for sale. Mr. Martinez helped Sofia choose the most appropriate one for the project, along with a few other electrical supplies. When Sofia hesitated at the extra charge for two-day delivery, Mr. Martinez squeezed her shoulders. "Don't worry, Sofia! It's for science!"

With her parents' supervision, Sofia worked on the wind turbine every night that week after school. Her father showed her how to use his power tools to cut the parts for the base and tower out of strong PVC plastic. He looked on to be sure she was handling the tools properly and carefully. Sofia cut the blades from poster board, glued them to the dowels, and pushed the free ends of the dowels into the slots in the little hub at the top of the turbine's tower. Mr. Martinez already had a battery in the basement, and they connected it to the mount with wires. When the motor and other supplies arrived, Sofia connected the motor and control system to the battery.

"Ready to launch!" she announced, carrying the turbine outside and setting it up on the crest of the hill in their backyard. Her parents followed.

Sure enough, as soon as the device was set up, the blades started to spin in the wind like a giant pinwheel. Sofia beamed as her project came to life.

While the turbine's blades spun faster and faster, Sofia hit the switch for the light bulb, and voilá! The filament inside the bulb began to flicker. Then it lit up fully, giving off a bright glow.

"You're a modern-day Thomas Edison!" Mrs. Martinez cried, clapping her hands.

Sofia hugged her parents. "Wait till I show this to Diya and Albert! They'll forget all about solar power and biofuel for our science project."

While Sofia had been telling her parents about her idea, Diya had been standing on the sidewalk looking at the gleaming solar panels that covered the roof of the Wilsons' house next door.

I bet the Espinoza twins could make solar panels out of old TV screens and a bunch of chicken wire, she thought, picturing the boy geniuses in lab coats and goggles, laboring away all night in a secret facility below the family garage. She came abruptly out of her daydream as Mr. Wilson stepped outside for his usual evening stroll. Diya's face brightened at the sight of him. Mr. Wilson had been her neighbor ever since she could remember, always ready to help when she struggled with difficult math and science homework.

Mr. Wilson greeted Diya pleasantly and they chatted for a moment about the solar panels. Diya explained her idea for the science fair.

"Ambitious!" said Mr. Wilson, impressed. "Maybe Freddie Ferrante at Simply Solar could help you out. He's the one who sold us our panels." He dug a card out of his wallet and handed it to her. "Here's his business card. He's such a nice guy. I'm sure he will be happy to help. Just tell him I told you to call."

Diya thanked Mr. Wilson and called the number on the card when she got home.

Diya was a bit nervous on the phone at first. Haltingly, she explained that she needed Mr. Ferrante's help because she wasn't simply working on a research paper, but an actual demonstration for the science fair. She wanted to show how solar energy could be used to power up a laptop at school. Heartened by Mr. Ferrante's obvious interest in the idea, she opened up a bit more.

"You see, I always work with Albert and Sofia, and I always go along with their ideas," she blurted out. "This time I have such a great idea of my own, and I think it will help us win first prize. And my neighbor Mr. Wilson says you guys are the best, so can you help?" she pleaded.

Diya heard a slight laugh on the other end, and then, "I'd be delighted to be a part of it. Can you come to the office tomorrow after school? We'll talk more about it and figure out a plan."

The next day after school, Ms. Mathur drove Diya to the Simply Solar office, a two-story brick building. Mr. Ferrante, a tall, burly middle-aged man with a kind face and a beard, stepped out and greeted them.

"Welcome to Simply Solar," he said, shaking hands with Diya and her mother. Diya's mom told her she'd be back in an hour. Mr. Ferrante then led Diya on a tour, showing her the models of different solar cell installations and asking questions about the science fair.

"We often set up solar panels on roofs like Mr. Wilson's," he explained, "but we do commercial installations as well. People are starting to realize the potential of solar power."

Diya, impressed with the displays, asked, "Just how do they work?"

"It's a simple process," Mr. Ferrante explained. "The cells in the panels absorb sunlight. A semiconductor inside the panels converts the sunlight into electricity. The panels are directly connected to the electrical grid, so the current goes through the regular utility company the homeowner uses."

Diya had never been a stellar science student, but being eager to please her teachers, she worked very hard in all her subjects. Her efforts paid off now because she understood everything Mr. Ferrante had said. Well, practically everything.

"But if the utility is supplying the electricity, how does solar power save money?" she asked.

"It's a convenient setup, actually," replied Mr. Ferrante. "The homeowner gets a credit for the solar power. The owner then uses the credit to pay for the electricity used at night or on overcast days when the sun isn't out and the panels don't work."

This made sense to Diya. Mr. Wilson had been right. Mr. Ferrante was a super-nice guy. He reminded her of Mr. Kowalski, with his explanations that were clear and easy to follow.

Mr. Ferrante asked Diya a few questions about her idea for the science fair and nodded. "You only need enough juice—that is, enough electricity—to power up a laptop," he concluded. "Look over here." He led Diya to a small, portable panel of cells. "A setup of this size will give you all the juice you need and then some, plus it's light and portable. You just need to set this by a window where it will get plenty of sunlight."

"How much does this panel cost?" Diya asked.

Mr. Ferrante smiled. "Normally, it'd run you in the hundreds of dollars, but for a good cause like science education, let's just call it a loan. After the science fair is over, you can bring it back. In return for the favor, I only ask that you display some of our business cards with your project—free publicity for us. But make sure it's all right with your principal first, of course. Or whichever teachers of yours are running the science fair."

"I'm sure the principal won't object," said Diya. "But I'll make sure to ask."

Mr. Ferrante showed Diya how to connect the solar panel to a small generator that would convert the solar energy into electricity. He explained that she would only have to plug the laptop into the generator.

A few minutes later, Diya thanked Mr. Ferrante profusely and headed outside. As always, her mother had shown up early and was sitting in the car reading the paper while she listened to the radio. Ms. Mathur looked in amazement at the box Sofia was setting gently on the back seat—a solar panel, a generator, and wires, as well as a smaller box of Simply Solar business cards.

As Ms. Mathur drove home, Diya chattered like a magpie about the equipment and her plans for the demonstration. She was thrilled to think that for once, the project idea would be hers. Maybe they had a good chance to beat the Espinozas and win first prize!

CHAPTER 4

A Surprising Turn

A week after they had met in the library, Diya, Albert, and Sofia sat around a big table in the chemistry lab, looking at one another. All three could barely contain their excitement and enthusiasm, but they tried to play it cool.

Diya had her laptop in front of her, Albert was holding a small motor in his hands, and Sofia had a block of wood on which she had attached a socket and a light bulb. A wire ran from the block across the room and out the open window.

"Who wants to go first?" asked Sofia. She was having a hard time concealing her impatience.

The three friends exchanged glances, and Albert spoke up first. "OK," he sighed. "Here goes nothing!"

He pointed to the shiny metal motor on the table, explaining that it was a small combustible engine that normally ran on gasoline. "Gasoline," Albert explained, "has too many down sides. It's expensive, it gives off harmful carbon dioxide, and it's made from petroleum, a nonrenewable form of energy, which means it will eventually run out."

As Albert continued explaining his idea, he grew more confident, and both Sofia and Diya were intrigued in spite of their resolutions to push for their own suggestions. Albert picked up Uncle Phil's jar of ethanol. He explained that it was cheaper and cleaner than gasoline, and that it was renewable since it was made of corn. "I've filled the motor's fuel tank with this precious liquid. So, will it run?" Albert paused for dramatic effect. "Drum roll, please!"

As Sofia rapidly drummed the edge of the table with both hands, Albert flicked a switch to start the motor. The engine sputtered briefly—and died. He tried again, producing only a screech from the motor. On the third try, the motor made no sound at all.

Albert was not only bewildered, but embarrassed. He knew the motor should have started because he had done exactly what Uncle Phil had said. He hated to look like a fool in front of his two best friends. Diya looked sympathetic, but at the same time Albert could see she was glad his idea hadn't worked. Sofia, whose support he could always count on, for once didn't understand how upset he was. "I guess this isn't the wave of the future," she said, grinning.

"Maybe the blend of the biofuel isn't right for a small engine," said Diya. "Call your uncle and ask him what's going on."

Albert nodded and shoved the motor aside. He was disappointed, but after all, it was more important to win first prize. He hoped one of the two girls had come up with something good!

Diya began explaining her solar-energy demonstration. "By the window you'll see a flat piece of metal," she explained. "It's a portable solar panel made up of many small solar cells. As I speak, the solar panel is absorbing the sun's rays, and the small generator you see is converting the solar energy into electricity. The generator is directly wired to my laptop. With just one little press of a button, I'll spark up this baby and you will stand amazed by the wonders of solar power!"

Diya pushed the laptop's *on* button and waited. The screen remained dark. She tried again. Nothing.

"Oops!" said Albert. He worked hard to suppress a grin. He had to admit to some relief at not being the only one whose idea had fizzled.

Sofia really felt bad. She had often tried to push Diya to be more forceful about contributing ideas and taking the lead in their group. She had been pleased at her friend's commitment to her own idea, even though it was a different plan from Sofia's. "Are all the connecting cords plugged in tight?" she asked, trying to be helpful.

Frowning anxiously, Diya carefully checked the connections. "Yes, everything

is in working order," she sighed. "I don't understand because it worked fine at home."

"Maybe the sun is closer to your house than it is to school," joked Albert.

As Diya ignored Albert and continued to fiddle with the wires, Sofia started her presentation. "I think my wind-energy project is going to blow you both away," she grinned.

"Ha, ha," sighed Albert wearily. He didn't appreciate Sofia's attempts at being funny.

"Let's see what you've got."

"If you look out the window, you'll see my wind turbine out there."

Albert and Diya got up and went to the window to get a closer look. Both were genuinely impressed. The small turbine looked good enough to have been built by the Espinozas! "Wow!" Albert said. "That's cool! Where did you buy it?"

"I didn't buy it; I made it," said Sofia proudly. She explained how her dad had

37

helped her find the necessary parts online, and shown her how to use his tools to build the turbine. Though Sofia had never been good at science tests, she always plunged happily into hands-on projects and lab work, often going beyond the limits of an assignment to bring in extra elements. Her enthusiasm helped all three of them get high marks on their group projects.

"I've attached the turbine to a small generator," Sofia said. "The converted electricity will light up this light bulb." As the turbine's blades spun, she flipped the switch on the wood block. The bulb lit up . . . and then went dark. Sofia flipped the switch again, but this time the bulb didn't light up at all.

The three friends looked at one another in dismay. Each had been so certain of impressing the others, and now it looked like none of them had a workable idea. Sofia was the most upset since she had been the most sure of success.

"We only have a week left before we have to tell Mr. Kowalski what our project is!" lamented Sofia. "We'll never finish something that works in time."

"Yeah," said Diya, "by now Kevin and Keith are probably mapping the surface of one of Jupiter's moons using a telescope made from old eyeglasses and paper-towel rolls!"

"We can't give up this easily," said Sofia. "We're smart, and we can solve problems."

Diya and Albert were reassured by her words. Sofia was the most practical of the three and good at making things happen when she put her mind to it. Albert was sure that if Sofia had confidence in the project, then she was right.

"We just need to put our heads together, figure out where we went wrong, and fix it," Sofia went on.

"Great idea!" said Albert. "Let's meet after school tomorrow at my house. We'll try to solve the problems together. How does that sound?"

"Sounds like a plan!" said Diya.

CHAPTER 5

Back on Track

It was four o'clock the next day when the three friends gathered after school at Albert's house with their science projects.

"Uncle Phil should be home from work any minute now," Albert said. "When he gets here, he should be able to tell us why the biofuel didn't work. While we're waiting, what's up with your solar panel, Diya?"

Diya explained that Mr. Ferrante was out of the office and would not be back until the following day. She looked worried. She didn't know enough about solar power to solve the mysterious failure without Mr. Ferrante's expert advice.

Sofia was convinced they could figure it out together if they tried. Albert especially was good at solving puzzles. Sofia reminded Diya that the experiment had worked at her home when she first tried it out. "Is there something wrong with the generator, maybe?"

"Unlikely," sighed Diya. "Mr. Ferrante wouldn't lend me a lemon."

Albert suddenly sat up straight and pushed up his glasses. "Wait, Diya! The sun was shining yesterday, and I assume all the parts were working. So maybe the solar cells in the panel just needed more time to absorb the sun's energy! How long after you set up the solar panel did you turn on your laptop?"

Diya thought for a moment. "I think it was about fifteen to twenty minutes," she said.

"That doesn't seem like enough time to me," said Albert. "Let's place it on the sill of the living room window. It's facing west and will get plenty of sun."

"OK, it's worth a try. I'm sure glad it's still sunny out," said Diya. "Let's leave it there for at least an hour and see if it makes any difference."

Just as they set up the solar panel on the windowsill, the front door opened and in walked Uncle Phil.

"Well, what do we have here—a Young Scientists of Tomorrow meeting?" he asked with a chuckle.

"Tomorrow won't be very bright if we don't get our science project together," said Diya mournfully.

"Oh? What's the problem?" asked Uncle Phil.

Albert pushed his glasses up again as he explained that all three of their demonstrations had failed. His words tumbled over each other as he asked about the failure of the biofuel.

Uncle Phil picked up the small motor, examined it, and laughed. "Well, the ethanol would've worked fine . . . if you had put it in the right motor," he said. "This is a diesel engine, Al. The ethanol will only work in a gas combustible engine."

Albert slapped his forehead. "You mean I picked up the wrong motor?"

"That's partly my fault," replied Uncle Phil. "I told you to grab the motor from my worktable, but there must have been two there. I need to organize the garage better. It's a mess!"

Uncle Phil led the group into the garage and to the motor on the worktable where he had left it. He opened the gas tank, and Albert carefully poured in some of the biofuel. When Albert flicked the switch, the engine purred like a contented kitten.

"It works!" he cried, and they all listened to the engine's hum for another minute until Uncle Phil shut it off.

The three friends returned to the house, leaving Uncle Phil to tidy things up in the chaotic garage.

"Well, that's one problem solved," said Albert. "Now what can we do about your wind turbine, Sofia?"

"I don't know," she said. "When I tried it at home, it worked perfectly. The electricity lit the bulb right up and it remained lit."

"That's really strange, Sof," said Diya. "Could it be that it was windier at your house than at school?"

Sofia mulled this over. "I did notice that the blades were spinning faster in my yard than at school, but I'm only a few blocks away from the school."

"But you've got a hill in your backyard," said Diya. "Don't wind turbines work best on hilltops where they catch more wind?"

"That's right!" Sofia said, her eyes wide. "At our house we put the turbine at the top of the little hill. At school it was on level ground and wasn't getting enough wind! Diya, you may be onto something!"

Albert asked Uncle Phil to drive them back to the school. They loaded Sofia's wind turbine into the back of his pickup truck and headed to Hillsdale High, where they carried the equipment to a hilltop on the other side of the building.

The blades of the turbine began to spin around, faster and faster, picking up greater speed until, finally, Sofia flicked the switch on the light bulb. It lit up almost immediately, as did her face.

"Success!" cried Sofia. "I am the Thomas Edison of wind! My wind turbine works."

"Congratulations, Sofia! But what about my project?" Diya interrupted. "Let's go back and check on my solar panel."

When they arrived back at Albert's house, Diya looked at her watch. "It's been about an hour and a half since we put the panel on the windowsill."

Diya sat down at the coffee table where she had set up her laptop. She closed her eyes, crossed her fingers, and pushed the laptop's *on* button.

Bwoing! The familiar sound of her laptop coming to life made Diya open her eyes and smile, and the screen lit up brightly, asking for her password.

"Genius!" she cried. "Espinoza twins, prepare to meet your doom!"

"So," said Sofia, after they'd all basked in the glory of their success for a while, "which kind of renewable energy are we choosing?"

"I don't know, Sof," said Albert. "Each of our demonstrations shows the power of renewable energy really, really well. It's a hard call."

The three of them looked at one another hesitantly. Now that they knew all three ideas worked, they weren't sure if they wanted to compromise. Albert liked the girls' ideas, but he felt that biofuel had the best chance of winning first place. Diya hated to give up when it seemed like her idea was the best of the three. Sofia was just about to voice her support for Diya's project when they heard Uncle Phil's voice.

"Why not use them all?" he called out from the kitchen, where he was fixing lemonade and sandwiches. "You've all worked very hard and these are three great ideas. I see no reason why you can't present all three as one project."

The friends were delighted with this suggestion. Albert was thrilled because if they had *three* demonstrations to the Espinozas' *one*, they were sure to win! Diya was pleased not to have to give up her idea, and Sofia thought it was a win-win situation in all ways. But then she frowned.

"If we want to win first prize, we need to really make our project stand out," she said. "I mean, lighting up one light bulb, powering a computer, and firing up a tiny motor aren't *that* impressive."

"Wait a minute," said Albert, leading his friends back to Uncle Phil's garage. "I think I've got an idea!"

CHAPTER 6

The Big Day

The high school gym was a flurry of activity on the morning of the science fair. Dozens of students were setting up demonstrations, display boards, and equipment on tables. There were science projects devoted to everything from water conservation to forensics to new methods of agriculture.

Albert, Diya, and Sofia were setting up their project at the far end of the gym near the rear door, which allowed people to get a glimpse of Sofia's wind turbine standing out on the hillside.

"We're going to win first prize, I just know it," said Albert. "These additions we've made will seal the deal."

Diya looked up from the display board where she was pinning up pages of explanatory text. "Everything's set to go," she said. "Espinoza twins, here we come!"

"And just in time too," said Sofia, gazing at the main doors as they burst open. In came a rush of students, faculty, family members, and friends. Leading the way were Mr. Kowalski, Principal Sanchez, and the other members of the science faculty who would serve as judges.

"I'm going to take a quick tour of the floor to assess our competition," said Albert.

"OK," said Sofia, "but don't be long. You need to help demonstrate when the judges get to us."

"Don't worry," Albert assured her. "I'll be back in plenty of time."

Diya and Sofia began explaining their project to a small group of several students and parents. Their explanation was thorough, and everyone seemed impressed. A few minutes later, Albert returned holding a paper lunch bag. He did not look happy.

"We're in trouble," he moaned, putting the bag down on the table.

RECYCLING

MONITORS GLASS PLASTIC

FAR OUT FORE

AGR

"Why?" asked Sofia.

"It's the Espinoza twins," Albert replied.

"I knew it!" groaned Diya. "What did they make—a hydroelectric dam out of old cereal boxes or something?"

"Well, no, not exactly," said Albert. "But they're not kidding around. Their exhibit looks amazing, and check these out." He showed his partners the contents of the paper bag—a charm bracelet and small notepad made from recycled materials, along with a magnet with pointers on how to live a "green" life. Albert looked sick. He had been so sure that their three-pronged project would win them the prize. But it appeared that Kevin and Keith had done them one better, as always. How could they possibly compete with gift bags of recycled stuff? Everyone liked getting free goodies.

Diya and Sofia looked at each other and at Albert in dismay. Then Diya rallied. "Come on, guys," she said. "Mr. Kowalski and the other judges aren't going to fall for a bunch of giveaways. We've got first prize in the bag!"

Albert, pushing his glasses into place, smiled at Diya's enthusiasm. He was starting to feel a little less deflated.

Sofia was the first to see the judges. "Are we ready?" she asked her friends. "You guys have all your stuff set up?"

As Albert and Diya assured her, Mr. Kowalski and Ms. Sanchez came up to them with a small group of faculty members. "Well, this looks like an ambitious project," said the principal.

"Please take your time to read the background information on solar energy, wind power, and biofuel," said Sofia. "And to make the reading easier, we'll cast a little more light on the subject."

With that, Sofia flicked a switch that lit up a string of small colored bulbs hanging above the display. "This light is provided courtesy of wind power," she explained. "It's generated by a wind turbine, which I built from information that I learned from my research online."

"Quite amazing," said Mrs. Pinsky, a biology teacher, who went outside to closely examine the turbine.

"This is interesting too," said Mr. Levesque, a physics teacher, pointing to a small wooden car that was zooming around the tabletop. On the table was a small billboard that read "Biofuel: The Fuel of the Future." Albert had made the car out of a carved block of wood, four toy wheels, and one of Uncle Phil's motors.

"The car is running on ethanol, made from corn oil," explained Albert. "A small amount of biofuel will keep the car running for about half an hour."

"Wow! I wish I could fill my gas guzzler with that stuff," said Ms. Sanchez. "Good job, Albert."

"Now, if you can take a moment to sit at one of these two laptop computers, we'd like you to type your thoughts about renewable energy," directed Diya.

Mr. Levesque pointed to the cords coming from the two laptops and exiting the rear gym door. "And what's the power source running these computers?"

"If you'll just look outside the door, you'll see, Mr. L," said Diya with a smile.

The judges gathered around the open door and looked out at the solar panel.

"The energy is provided courtesy of solar power," she explained, "generated by the portable solar panel outside. Amazing, huh?"

"Very impressive," said Mr. Kowalski.

The rest of the afternoon passed by quickly. The three friends demonstrated their project for one group of students, parents, and friends after another. Most people also took the time to type something using the laptops. Ms. Mathur, Mr. and Mrs. Martinez, and Uncle Phil all beamed with pride when they stopped by the exhibit.

Diya was pleased to see many adults taking the Simply Solar business cards she had placed on the table. She wasn't so thrilled that they were dropping the cards inside bags they'd picked up from Kevin and Keith. She lost heart even more when she visited the twins' exhibit, which was pretty amazing. Visitors were sitting on benches made of recycled plastic bottles, light twinkled through stained glass windows made from recycled glass, and a row of recycled computer monitors showed recycling in action.

At three o'clock, Mr. Kowalski picked up a microphone and asked everyone to gather in the center of the gym.

"The judges have deliberated. I'm very pleased to announce we have decided on the three winning science projects," he said.

"The suspense is killing me," Sofia nervously whispered to Diya.

"I know," admitted Diya. "Do you want to accept the prize or should I?"

"I can say that everyone who created a project is a winner," continued Mr. Kowalski, "but contests being what they are, we had the difficult task of picking the three we felt were the best ones. So, without any further ado, third prize goes to . . ."

Albert held his breath while Diya squeezed Sofia's hand.

". . . Lisa Gibbons and Robin O'Neill for their project on water conservation!"

The two students made their way through the crowd to shake hands with Mr. Kowalski and Principal Sanchez and receive their award letter and trophy.

"Two more chances," said Sofia softly.

"And second prize goes to . . ." began Mr. Kowalski.

"I think I'm going to be sick," gasped Albert.

"Keith and Kevin Espinoza," said Mr. Kowalski, "for their outstanding presentation on recycling!"

The twins walked up to receive their prize and handshakes, and Albert couldn't help noticing that their smiles were somewhat forced. Keith and Kevin were so used to winning all the top prizes in science. He felt a pang of sympathy for them. After all, their project had looked great.

"Before I announce our first prize winners, I just want to say that the issue this team chose is an especially critical one facing our community today. Their cutting-edge project demonstrated a wide range of renewable energy—solar energy, wind power, and biofuel. First prize of this year's science fair goes to Diya Mathur, Sofia Martinez, and Albert Carney!"

Everyone clapped and cheered as the three friends went up to get their prize. As Ms. Sanchez shook Sofia's hand, she leaned over and said, "I'd like to talk to you three afterward, Sofia. Can you meet me in my office in fifteen minutes?"

Sofia nodded, wondering what the principal wanted to talk about.

As people crowded around to congratulate them, Diya saw a familiar face. It was Mr. Ferrante. She beamed at him and shook hands enthusiastically as he congratulated her on the project.

"Thank you," said Diya. "But I have another favor to ask. I need to keep the panel for a few more days—the science fair stays open till Tuesday."

"No need to worry about returning it at all," said Mr. Ferrante. "Consider it a gift."

Diya's eyes widened. "I thought you were just lending it to me!" she exclaimed.

"Let's just say you've earned it," explained Mr. Ferrante. "You see, I just talked to Principal Sanchez, who is so impressed by your project that she wants to propose the possibility of Hillsdale High going solar. She wants me to make a presentation to the school board next week."

"That's fantastic!" cried Diya.

After Mr. Ferrante said good-bye, Diya went with Albert and Sofia to Ms. Sanchez's office. The principal was sitting at her desk, hands folded in front of her, with Mr. Kowalski in a chair across the room.

"Sit down, please," Ms. Sanchez told them. "You three have made a great case for renewable energy. I think it's time our school joined other businesses in town and started exploring alternative sources of energy. I've already talked to Mr. Ferrante about the possibility of installing solar panels on our roof to supply electricity to the school."

"We heard!" said Diya. "Mr. Ferrante just told us."

"We're excited to work with him," continued the principal, "but your project got me thinking about other ways we can use renewable energy here at Hillsdale. I envision us using biofuel in our lawn mowers and other equipment, and perhaps we could install a few small wind turbines on the hillside. Imagine a whole interactive installation that teaches students, benefits the entire school community, *and* cuts costs for Hillsdale! Of course, since you started all this with your science project, you three would serve as consultants and work with the science faculty. What do you say?"

"Yes!" the friends blurted out in unison.

As they left the principal's office, Albert said, "Well, I guess we finally proved which form of renewable energy is best, didn't we?"

"We sure did," Diya said with a sly smile.

"Without a doubt," Sofia laughed, and the three friends hurried back to the gym to share the exciting news with their families.